W9-BLX-677

The Denesuline

CAROL KOOPMANS

Weigl

CALGARY
www.weigl.com

Published by Weigl Educational Publishers Limited
6325 10 Street SE
Calgary, Alberta, Canada
T2H 2Z9

Website: www.weigl.com

Library and Archives Canada Cataloguing in Publication Data

Koopmans, Carol
    Denesuline / Carol Koopmans.
(Canadian Aboriginal art and culture)
Includes index.
ISBN 978-1-55388-345-6 (bound)
ISBN 978-1-55388-346-3 (pbk.)
    1. Chipewyan Indians--Juvenile literature. I. Title. II. Series.
E99.C59K66 2007   j971.004'972   C2007-902195-6

Printed in Canada
1 2 3 4 5 6 7 8 9 0 11 10 09 08 07

Project Coordinator Heather Kissock   **Design** Janine Vangool   **Validator** Karyn Sharp, University of Northern British Columbia

Photograph Credits
Every reasonable effort has been made to trace ownership and to obtain permission to reprint copyright material. The publishers would be pleased to have any errors or omissions brought to their attention so that they may be corrected in subsequent printings.

Cover (main): © Canadian Museum of Civilization (VI-D-259, S92-2544); **Cover (top left):** NWT Archives (N-1995-002:7095); © **Canadian Museum of Civilization:** pages 3 (VI-D-5, D2005-12275), 7 (VI-D-114, D2003-11550), 11 left (VI-D-279, D2003-11222), 11 right (VI-D-259, S92-2544), 14 (VI-D-227 a-b, D2003-11518), 20 (VI-D-84 a-b, D2003-11518), 24 top (VI-D-5, D2005-12275), 24 bottom (VI-D-33 a-b, S93-734), 30 (VI-D-84 a-b, D2003-11518); **Glenbow Archives:** page 6 (NA-1700-96); **Courtesy of Alex Janvier:** page 27; **NWT Archives:** pages 1 (N-1995-002:7095), 9 (G-1995-001-8004), 10 (G-1995-001-8088), 15 (N-1979-051-0360s), 17 (G-1995-001-5497), 18 (N-1995-002:7103), 19 (N-1995-002:6610), 21 (N-1995-002:7095), 22 (N-1995-002:1572).

We acknowledge the financial support of the Government of Canada through the Book Publishing Industry Development Program (BPIDP) for our publishing activities.

Please note
All of the Internet URLs given in the book were valid at the time of publication. However, due to the dynamic nature of the Internet, some addresses may have changed, or sites may have ceased to exist since publication. While the author and publisher regret any inconvenience this may cause readers, no responsibility for any such changes can be accepted by either the author or the publisher.

CONTENTS

The People

Thousands of years before Europeans began exploring northern Canada, this huge land mass was home to **First Nations** peoples. Many of these groups lived in an area that extended across the northern part of Canada from Labrador west to British Columbia. These groups are called the People of the **Subarctic**. The Denesuline are one of the largest First Nations groups living in the subarctic.

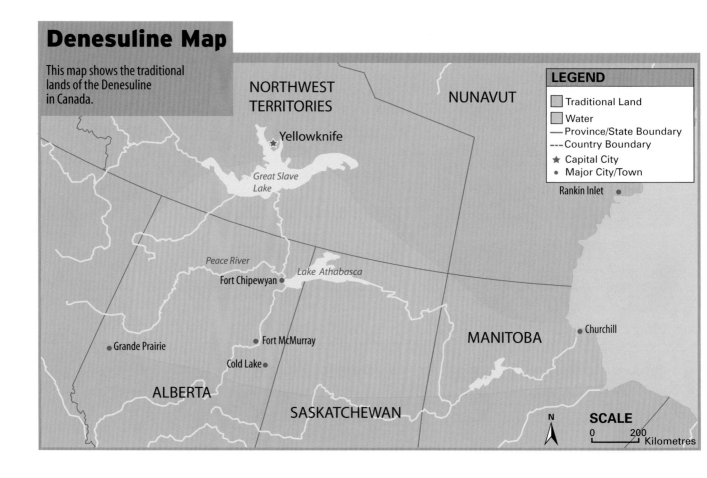

Denesuline Map

This map shows the traditional lands of the Denesuline in Canada.

NORTHWEST TERRITORIES

NUNAVUT

★ Yellowknife

Great Slave Lake

LEGEND
- ☐ Traditional Land
- ☐ Water
- — Province/State Boundary
- --- Country Boundary
- ★ Capital City
- • Major City/Town

Rankin Inlet •

Peace River

Lake Athabasca

Fort Chipewyan •

• Churchill

MANITOBA

• Grande Prairie

• Fort McMurray

Cold Lake •

ALBERTA

SASKATCHEWAN

N

SCALE
0   200
Kilometres

The subarctic area has a range of landforms. Much of the subarctic is barren, nearly flat land called tundra. Most of the subarctic is covered with forest, rivers, and hundreds of small lakes. Summers are short, and the winters are very cold. The Denesuline's survival depended on their ability to live in this environment. Nature provided the means for all food, clothing, and shelter.

MODERN LIVING

Today, the Denesuline live in towns and cities in the Northwest Territories, as well as in northern Alberta, Saskatchewan, and the Hudson Bay area of northern Manitoba. Many also live on **reserves**. The Denesuline are working hard to keep their traditional **culture** alive. They celebrate their history by practising traditional beliefs, reviving Denesuline language skills, and collecting their **elders**' stories.

Many Denesuline live around Great Slave Lake, in the Northwest Territories.

Denesuline Homes

The Denesuline moved with the seasons in search of edible plants and game. Homes had to be easy to put together, take apart, and move. The Denesuline relied on teepees or ridge-pole lodges for this reason.

Teepees were built using animal skins that were stretched over tree poles. The skins covered the teepee's frame and provided protection from the weather. A smoke flap at the top controlled the flow of fresh air. A small opening with a hide over it served as a door. Rolling the lower side flaps up allowed cool breezes to flow in and out. Heavy stones and wooden pegs placed around the edge held everything in place.

Ridge-pole lodges, or "lean-tos," were constructed for use as shelter on short hunting, fishing, or trapping trips. The lodges were quick to build. They had a two-sided pole frame that looked like an upside-down "V." Mats made of woven leaves, hides, or bark covered the poles and filled the gaps between them.

Denesuline homes were suited to the weather. The Denesuline often lived in teepees in the spring. These were covered with waterproof animal skins, keeping the inside dry during rainstorms.

WINTER DWELLING

The Denesuline used wigwams as their winter homes. Wigwams had a more rounded dome shape than a teepee. The dome-shaped frame consisted of long, thin poles set into holes in the ground. Each pole was part of a pair, with each pair curving to form an arch that met at the top. Tightly tied strips of animal hide bound each pair together. Several pairs of poles formed this dome frame.

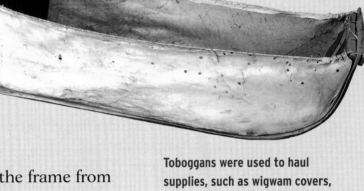

Toboggans were used to haul supplies, such as wigwam covers, from camp to camp in the winter. They were often pulled by dog teams.

The Denesuline made coverings for the frame from bark, animal furs, or mats of leaves that were tightly stitched together. Bark was lightweight, resistant to water, and easy to use, if available.

Inside the wigwam, furs or branches often covered the ground. A fire in the centre was used for providing warmth and cooking. Rocks circled the fire to prevent it from spreading. A hole in the dome roof allowed smoke from the campfire to escape. A flap covered the smoke hole. People entered and left the wigwam by crawling through a small opening with a cover.

Often, when the Denesuline moved camps, they took the wigwam coverings with them, leaving the frame for their return. The coverings were light and easy to carry as they moved from camp to camp.

Denesuline Communities

Everyone played an important role in a Denesuline community. Survival depended on cooperation from all members in the camp. Men did the hunting and scouting for food. This often took them away from the camp in search of moose or caribou. Some, however, remained behind to protect their camp.

Camp life was family-centred. Children learned by watching and doing. They worked alongside family members to learn practical skills. Girls helped their mothers with collecting roots and berries, or with fishing. Girls also learned about food preparation, making clothing, moving camps, and caring for children. Boys learned to track, hunt, trap, and fish from their fathers and the other men of the group. These skills were important for finding food and shelter.

The caribou was the most important animal to the Denesuline's survival. Boys learned to hunt these animals, while girls learned how to prepare the meat for food and the hides for clothing.

The Denesuline thought the act of sharing was more important than having wealth in possessions. Each person earned respect by showing respect for others. Denesuline men had to provide for their family. If a man shared the family's food and possessions with others, he gained respect. Denesuline leaders were chosen for their courage, wisdom, willingness to listen, or a special skill.

The Denesuline did not use any formal leadership or chief. They did not have a system for electing or choosing leaders. Rather than a single leader, the leadership role was shared. It was given to the person best suited for the job that needed doing. For example, when scouting wildlife, the best tracker led the others.

Shared leadership allowed many to take a turn as leader. The people with the required skills either volunteered, or the group chose them to lead. In this way, each person gained respect and recognition. This prevented any single person from gaining too much control.

Today, elders take the time to teach and supervise their youth in the traditional ways of the Denesuline. Food preparation is just one of the traditions being passed to younger generations.

Denesuline Clothing

Most Denesuline clothing was made from animal hides. Before the women could make clothing, the hides had to be prepared for use. First, the women used a **bone beamer** to scrape hair away from the raw hides. Next, the hides were soaked in a mixture of water and caribou brains to soften them. More scraping, stretching, rubbing, and smoking completed the process. The hides were then ready to be made into clothing.

The Denesuline wore a variety of clothes, including coats, shirts, parkas, leggings, and mittens. Men and women wore the same style of clothing. Two-piece outfits, consisting of pants and a long-sleeved top, were typical. Men's tops had a pointed shirt tail on the front and back. Women's tops were pointed in the back but had a straight front. Women's parkas had extra room in the back to allow for carrying a child. Up to 10 moose or caribou hides could be used to create one winter outfit.

Preparing clothes was a highly skilled task in which Denesuline women took great pride.

The Denesuline wore moccasins, or soft leather shoes, on their feet. Moccasins had to be strong and sturdy to survive the active Denesuline lifestyle. Moose skin was used because of its strength, while fur served as decorative trim and helped to keep snow out of the insides of peoples' shoes.

The Denesuline carried dried food and valuable items in rectangular, laced sacs called *babiches.* These bags were made from the skin of caribou forelegs. As with clothing, the hair of the caribou was removed from the skin. The skin was dried and cut into long, narrow strips. These strips were made into a bag. Often porcupine quillwork, fringes, and embroidery added beauty and decoration to the bag.

Denesuline women added decorative features to most of the clothing and accessories they made.

Denesuline clothing today often features the traditional floral designs of the past.

Denesuline Food

Caribou are found across the subarctic region of Canada. These animals served as the main food source for the Denesuline. No part of a caribou went to waste. The animals provided most of life's needs for food, shelter, and clothing. Meat cut into strips was dried and stored for later use. Caribou leg skins became bags for meat storage. The intestines served as containers for fat, grease, or **pemmican**.

Men hunted in the forest areas or woodlands for caribou, bear, and moose. Traps were set to catch small game, such as beavers and rabbits. Nets made from raw caribou skins or willow bark were cast in freshwater streams to catch trout, pike, and whitefish.

When in season, women picked wild berries, including blueberries, saskatoons, cranberries, and raspberries. Women smoked or sun-dried meat, fish, and berries to preserve for later eating. Drying food could preserve it for an entire year.

Huckleberries were an important part of the Denesuline diet. These berries could be used to make pemmican, dried for later, or mashed to make juice.

Pemmican Cakes

Ingredients

1 package beef jerky

0.24 litre dried berries

0.24 litre chopped nuts or sunflower seeds

60 millilitres beef suet or vegetable shortening

honey to taste

Equipment

12-cup muffin tin

knife

paper liners

saucepan

wooden spoon

1. Line muffin cups with paper liners.

2. Chop beef jerky into confetti-sized pieces to make about 0.24 L. Melt suet or shortening in a saucepan.

3. Remove from heat, stir in beef jerky, dried berries, and seeds. Stir in honey.

4. Spoon about 60 mL of the pemmican mixture into each muffin cup. Press down firmly to make a cake, smoothing the top.

5. Refrigerate until set, and then, enjoy.

Denesuline Tools

The Denesuline used tools to secure food and build shelters. Tools made from stone, bones, and wood helped people complete all tasks in their daily life.

Men carried basic tools made out of stone. Following European contact, they used hatchets, files, and knives. In winter, they used ice chisels for chopping through ice. Strips of caribou hide were braided to become laces for snowshoes, fishing nets, and bags.

Women's tools included spoons and ladles for food preparation. These utensils were made from wood and horns. Antlers were carved into finely crafted knives. Women cooked using containers made from caribou skin or bark. Strips of bark from birch trees were shaped into bowls. Tree roots were woven into baskets. Moose and caribou bones became needles, scrapers, or **awls** for sewing.

The Denesuline used snowshoes to help them walk across deep snow. Snowshoes stopped them from sinking in snow during a hunt.

CARIBOU HUNTING

The Denesuline used different methods to hunt caribou. Some hunters caught caribou by using snares. Other hunters used bows and arrows. In some subarctic regions, hunters speared caribou as they crossed rivers during their **migration** each year.

Caribou fences formed another type of trap. Construction was a major undertaking and required several families to cooperate. Using logs, brush, or rocks, people built miles of fences. The fences were shaped into V-shaped pathway. The Denesuline herded the caribou along this pathway and steered them into a corral.

With the arrival of European traders to the subarctic, guns gradually replaced traditional forms of hunting. Still, caribou continues to be an important food source for the Denesuline.

In the past, caribou fences were made using stone markers. Later, fence posts and barbed wire were used.

Denesuline Religion

The Denesuline had great respect for nature. They lived in harmony with their surroundings and believed that everything in the universe had a spirit. This spirituality, or *Inkonze*, connected all things. Spiritual powers came to people through dreams or visions. Anyone having these dreams was believed to have spiritual power.

The Denesuline believed that animals had spirits, and some animals held special powers. The eagle carried the prayers of the people to the Great Spirit. Eagles were sacred, and hunters did not kill them.

Medicine people acted as the spiritual guides of the group. They communicated with guard spirits, who appeared in their dreams in the form of animals. During the dreams, guard spirits provided medicine people with guidance and direction. Using stories, medicine people told people of these dreams. These stories helped people to understand the world around them.

Medicine people were treated with great respect. It was their job to hold off evil and calm the spirits. Medicine people gave strict orders to try to keep the spirits happy. They told men to follow certain rituals when making their fish nets. They were to weave the nets exactly the same way each time they made them in order to satisfy the spirits.

Often, a medicine person was expected to be a healer who helped people physically and spiritually. At some time in his or her life, a Denesuline might participate in a **vision quest**. It was the medicine person's role to guide the person through the vision quest.

Spirituality was applied to all aspects of Denesuline life. Prior to a fishing trip, medicine people would perform specific ceremonies to ensure that the fishers would come back with a good catch.

Ceremonies and Celebrations

The Denesuline based their celebrations on the stories of their medicine people. They did not take part in formal religious ceremonies. All of life was considered a prayerful act.

Social gatherings were generally held in the summer and winter to mark major events in life, such as births, marriages, and death. Large gatherings and feasts were held during the **eclipse** of the Moon, to welcome visitors, and to celebrate reunions and partings. All gatherings followed the same format. Celebrations included speeches, stories, feasting, praying, singing, dancing, and drumming.

The Dene National Assembly is held every year. This event gives all Dene groups, including the Denesuline, the opportunity to celebrate their culture and discuss the issues facing them.

With the exploration of northern Canada in the early 1700s, the **Roman Catholic** church sent priests to remote regions. Some Denesuline chose to become Catholic. Others continued to practise traditional spirituality. Today, social gatherings remain central to Densuline life. **Christian** celebrations, such as Christmas and Easter, are celebrated regularly.

The crucifix, or cross, is an important symbol in the Catholic faith. It symbolizes the sacrifice of Jesus Christ.

MARRIAGE

In most cases, Denesuline marriages were arranged by parents. The couple involved often had little say in who they married. A daughter could refuse the man chosen for her, but this happened only on rare occasions. Generally, the offer of marriage was made by fathers, but mothers made the decision. Grandparents also carried much influence in deciding who young people would marry. Once parents agreed to a match, they told the community leader, who announced it at a ceremony that the entire community attended.

During the wedding ceremony, the couple was given advice by community elders. They were told how to take care of each other and what their responsibilities were in the marriage. Following this, the couple would thank the elders. Shouts of joy would blend with the beating of drums as the community celebrated the couple's marriage.

Denesuline Music

Singing and drumming have been at the core of First Nations celebrations for thousands of years. Drums are used to accompany singing and dancing. Men sit in a circle around the drum. Drumming begins by the men striking the drum in unison with a covered mallet. The rhythmic beating and singing draws listeners of all ages. Drums are made of animal hide stretched on a round wooden frame. To improve the quality of the sound when struck, the rawhide is softened over an open fire. It is then stretched to fit the drum.

Over the past century, Scottish and French-Canadian music from explorers, fur traders, and trappers has become part of many Denesuline celebrations. Fiddling, square dancing, and jigging are now a recognized part of the Denesuline musical **heritage**.

Drums made from caribou skin have become a symbol of the Dene. These drums are still used in ceremonies today.

POWWOWS

Powwows are gatherings that usually include feasting, drumming, and dancing. They can occur as part of a social event, a meeting, or a conference. While powwows were not originally part of traditional Denesuline celebrations, today they have been adopted and are part of many Denesuline occasions.

Powwows include drum dancing. Dancers move in a circle around the drummers, who sit in the centre. Everyone is welcome to join in the circle dances and step to the rhythm of the drum beat. Age-old steps have changed little from generation to generation. Many people also learn new dances when visiting other groups.

Drumming is traditionally done by men. Today, women are beginning to drum as well and have even formed successful drumming groups.

Language and Storytelling

The Denesuline belong to the Athapaskan language group. Besides the Denesuline, the Athapaskan languages include the Beaver, Dogrib, Hare, and Slave First Nations. The Denesuline speak a language also called Denesuline.

Denesuline is still spoken in many **dialects** across northern Canada, but there are less than 4,000 Denesuline who speak the language. The federal government considers the Denesuline language to be **endangered**. Denesuline elders have voiced concerns that children are no longer

Events such as the Dene National Assembly give the Denesuline an opportunity to speak their traditional language.

DAGHIDA

Storytelling is an important part of Denesuline culture. In the past, stories were often told around a campfire. Storytelling was a way to gather and give information. It was the way people learned lessons about life. Stories were passed from grandparents to parents to children.

The Denesuline do not want their culture and language to disappear. Efforts to restore the Denesuline language are underway. In 2000, the *Daghida* project began in Cold Lake, Alberta. The Denesuline word *Daghida* means "we are alive." The aim of the project is to keep the Denesuline language alive by teaching children to speak it. The project was planned in three stages. First, the language was researched. Then, language teachers were trained. Finally, the project moved into the schools. Denesuline children are now taught to speak the Denesuline language. Projects such as this may help restore the Denesuline language and keep it alive.

In Denesuline mythology, the wolverine represents determination and self worth.

Denesuline Art

The Denesuline express themselves through many forms of art. Women weave baskets, stitch embroidery, and apply porcupine quills to clothes for decoration. Men craft carvings. These special skills and efforts are prized. Artists earn respect through their hard work and beautiful creations.

Porcupine quillwork is an ancient art form. Women practised it long before European materials, such as glass beads, became available. To prepare the porcupine quills for quilling, they were pounded until they were flat. The quills were then coloured with natural dyes from plants and flowers. Women wove the stained quills into animal hides to add texture, colour, and interest to their clothes.

Dene women are known for their colourful beadwork and silk embroidery.

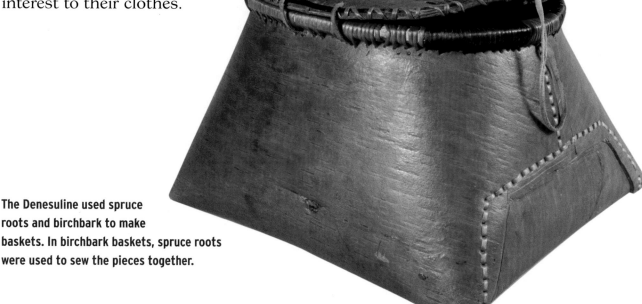

The Denesuline used spruce roots and birchbark to make baskets. In birchbark baskets, spruce roots were used to sew the pieces together.

Basket weaving is an art form that is centuries old. Learning the skill of weaving took practice and patience. To make baskets, women used materials found in the regions where they lived, such as spruce roots. Few tools were required. Once the roots were woven into basket shapes, colourful designs were added using dyes made from berries or roots.

Finding spruce roots for basketmaking was a dirty activity. Denesuline women would head into the woods, where they would look for young roots extending from spruce trees. When they found a root, they would use a digging stick, often an antler, to unearth and follow the root to its tip. Some spruce roots could be up to 6 metres long. Once the root was taken from the tree, the person would thank the tree for its contribution. Then, the bark was removed, and the root was coiled in order to prepare it for use.

Before roots could be used for weaving baskets, they had to be split. This involved cutting into the end of the root and splitting it down the centre. This process could be repeated a few times until the weaver had the strips required for the project.

Baskets made from spruce roots were once very common in Denesuline homes. They were replaced with containers, such as copper pots, when the Europeans arrived. The Denesuline are now trying to bring back the craft of traditional basketmaking through classes and workshops.

Thanadelthur

Thanadelthur was a Denesuline woman who helped the **Hudson's Bay Company** expand the fur trade. In 1713, as a teenager, Thanadelthur was captured by the Cree. With the help of some fur traders, she escaped and made her way to the York Factory trading post. There, Thanadelthur told the traders that the Denesuline wanted to trade furs with them. She also told the traders about the abundance of furs beyond the Churchill River.

The Hudson's Bay Company relied heavily on Aboriginal Peoples. Not only did they supply furs to the company, they also acted as guides, interpreters, and teachers of survival skills.

The traders organized a voyage to map and explore the area. They asked Thanadelthur to act as their guide. The group embarked on a journey that took almost a year. During the journey, they were attacked by the Cree, but Thanadelthur convinced the Cree and Denesuline to make peace.

On her return to York Factory, Thanadelthur taught the Denesuline which furs the British most valued. She showed them how to prepare the furs to get the highest price. Although she died of a fever the next winter, Thanadelthur's role in the mission earned her respect from both **Aboriginal Peoples** and British fur traders.

MODERN ARTIST

Alex Janvier

Alex Janvier is one of Canada's leading artists. Born in 1935, Alex is Denesuline and from Alberta's Cold Lake First Nation. At the age of 8, he was sent to the Blue Quills Indian **Residential School**. During his years at the residential school, Alex explored his artistic interests and began to create paintings and other artwork. After graduating from the Alberta College of Art in Calgary, in 1960, Alex began teaching art at the University of Alberta.

Alex credits the traditional beadwork and birchbark basketry of his mother and others as inspiration for his art. His artistry is a unique blending of the real with the **abstract**. Alex chooses bold and symbolic colours to express both the struggles and successes he has experienced. Many of his paintings are in the form of murals, which are painted on walls and ceilings. Alex's murals can be found in institutions such as the Canadian Museum of Civilization in Gatineau, Quebec.

Over the years, Alex's work has been presented in dozens of major exhibitions, including shows in countries such as Sweden and France. He has received great honours and recognition. Alex has been awarded lifetime achievement awards from the National Aboriginal Achievement Foundation, The Tribal Chiefs Institute, and Cold Lake First Nation. In 1998, he was hired by the Royal Canadian Mint to design a white bison for the $200 coin.

On September 6, 2003, Alex and his family opened an art gallery in Cold Lake, Alberta, featuring Alex's work. A website devoted to his art was created in 2004. In 2007, Alex was awarded the Order of Canada.

The bright, intense colours used by Alex, like the blues in "Eagle Clarion," make his art unique and eye-catching. Alex's paintings are often symbolic of his culture and history.

Studying the Past

Archaeologists collect information from the past by digging through layers of earth and finding remains of items people have left behind. These **artifacts** provide clues to the past. Archaeologists also study written records and talk to elders to learn about Denesuline culture.

People living in the Canadian subarctic have an ancient history. Based on their studies and the artifacts they have found, archaeologists have found items of Aboriginal **ancestors** in the Canadian subarctic that date back as many as 8,000 to 12,000 years ago.

Items left behind by the Denesuline, such as tools, weapons, or clothing, help archaeologists determine how these people lived thousands of years ago.

TIMELINE

8,000-12,000 years ago

Humans are known to have occupied the northern prairie region of what is now Canada.

1620s

Initial European contact with the Denesuline is established.

1689

The Hudson's Bay Company attempts to establish trading relationships with the Denesuline by constructing a trading post at the mouth of the Churchill River, in present-day Manitoba.

1715

Trade between the Denesuline and the Hudson's Bay Company is firmly established.

1780s-1790s

The Hudson's Bay Company establishes trading posts along the Denesuline's southern borders.

1781-1783

A disease called smallpox kills 90 percent of the Denesuline population.

1899

The Denesuline sign a **treaty** with the federal government that grants them hunting and fishing rights as well as reserve land.

1970

The Indian Brotherhood of the Northwest Territories is created to protect the rights and interests of the Denesuline.

1990

Dene languages become official languages of the Northwest Territories.

The Churchill River empties into Hudson Bay, one of the key transportation routes for the fur trade.

Make a Drum and Mallet

The drum plays an important role in Denesuline spirituality and culture. You can share this experience by making your own drum and mallet.

Materials

2 balloons

embroidery ring or other circular frame

2 elastic bands

piece of cloth

stick or branch (1.25 centimetres in diameter and 30 centimetres long)

paints for decorating (optional)

1. Cut the bottom off one of the balloons.

2. Stretch the balloon over the top of the frame, and secure it with an elastic band.

3. Decorate the drum using the paints.

4. Cut the bottom off the other balloon. Stuff the cloth into the end of the balloon to make a small ball.

5. Place the stick in the stuffed balloon. Gather the ends of the balloon around the stick, and fasten them with the other elastic band.

6. Now, your drum and mallet are ready to make music.

Further Reading

Find out more about spruce-root basketry in *Long-Ago People's Packsack, Whadqq Tehmi: Dene Babiche Bags, Tradition and Revival* (Canadian Museum of Civilization, 2005).

Photographs and descriptions of Denesuline clothing can be found in Judy Thompson's *From the Land: Two Hundred Years of Dene Clothing* (Canadian Museum of Civilization, 1995).

Websites

The past, present, and future of the Denesuline are explored at **www.sicc.sk.ca/heritage/ethnography/dene/origin/index.html**.

Learn about the efforts being made to save the Dene language at **http://jan.ucc.nau.edu/~jar/NALI3.html**.

To read more about the traditional clothing of the Denesuline, visit **www.civilization.ca/aborig/threads/thred10e.html**.

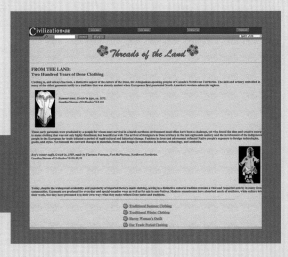

GLOSSARY

INDEX

Aboriginal Peoples: the original or earliest known inhabitants of what is now Canada

abstract: having to do with a style of art that does not show real objects, but uses lines, shapes, and colours to suggest an idea or feeling

ancestors: relatives who lived a very long time ago

archaeologists: scientists who study objects from the past to learn about people who lived long ago

artifacts: items, such as tools, made by a human

awls: sharp tools used for making holes in soft materials

bone beamer: an ancient tool made from bone; used in scraping hides

Christian: practising a religion based on the teachings of Jesus Christ

culture: the arts, beliefs, habits, and institutions considered as being characteristic of a specific community, people, or nation

dialects: variations on a language that is spoken in a certain place

eclipse: a blocking out of light

elders: the older and more influential people of a group or community

endangered: at risk of no longer living on Earth

First Nations: members of Canada's Aboriginal community who are not Inuit or Métis

heritage: the people, places, and culture of the past

Hudson's Bay Company: a trading company that played a major role in the exploration and development of Canada

migration: to move from one place to another because of the weather

pemmican: a mixture of dried meat and berries that has been pounded into powder and mixed with fat

reserves: land set aside for First Nations groups by the Canadian government

residential school: a boarding school for Aboriginal students set up by the federal government

Roman Catholic: a Christian religion that governed by the pope

subarctic: a huge land region stretching across the upper part of northern Canada

treaty: an agreement between two nations

vision quest: a spiritual journey